SUPERCARS

MEAN MACHINES

PAUL HARRISON

Arcturus

This edition first published in 2012 by Arcturus Publishing

Distributed by Black Rabbit Books
P. O. Box 3263
Mankato
Minnesota MN 56002

Copyright © 2012 Arcturus Publishing Limited

Printed in China

Library of Congress Cataloging-in-Publication Data

Harrison, Paul, 1969-
 Supercars / by Paul Harrison.
    p. cm. -- (Mean machines)
 Includes index.
 ISBN 978-1-84858-564-5 (hardcover, library bound)
 1. Automobiles, Racing--Juvenile literature. 2. Sports cars--Juvenile literature. I. Title.
 TL236.H37 2013
 629.228--dc23

2011051436

Text: Paul Harrison
Editor: Joe Harris
Design: sprout.uk.com
Cover design: sprout.uk.com

Picture credits:
Corbis: 7 (Leo Mason), 26 (Car Culture), 27t (Car Culture), 27b (Car Culture). Magic Pictures:
10–11. Mercedes-Benz: 16t, 16b, 17t, 17b. Offside/L'Equipe: 6b. Shutterstock: all cover images,
3, 4, 5t, 5b, 6t, 8b, 28–29, 29t. www.carphoto.co.uk: 12–13, 14t, 14b, 15, 24, 25. www.pagani.com:
20t, 20b, 21. www.shelbysupercars.com: 22–23, 22b. www.teslamotors.com/roadster: 30–31, 31t,
31b. www.thrustssc.com: 8–9c, 9. www.xenatecgroup.com: 18–19, 18b.

SL002135US

SUPERCARS

CONTENTS

BUGATTI VEYRON SUPER SPORT

Some cars stand out from the crowd. They are faster, more expensive, and better to drive than other cars. In short, they are **supercars**—and they don't come any more super than the Bugatti Veyron SSC.

Nothing comes cheap on the Bugatti. An annual service at the garage will cost $42,000.

The body is made of carbon fiber, which is incredibly light but very strong.

Braking at high speed can cause normal brakes to fail. The Super Sport uses brakes made of porcelain instead. Porcelain copes with heat better than metal brakes.

The speed has been restricted on road models to 258 mph (415 km/h) in order to save the tires from being destroyed. As it costs $27,700 for a set of tires, this is probably a good idea.

What makes the Bugatti Veyron SSC a supercar? For a start it is the fastest production car in the world. It can accelerate to 60 mph (100 km/h) in 2.5 seconds and has an incredible top speed of nearly 262 mph (421km/h)!

You'll need deep pockets to buy a Super Sport. Only five Super Sports were made and they each sell for an incredible $2.2 million!

A wing pops out of the back of the car when it reaches 113 mph (182 km/h). The wing uses the wind to push the car down to help it grip the road.

The powerful engine was designed for speed and not fuel economy. The Super Sport does a measly 6.4 miles per gallon (37 l per 100 km) when driving around town.

SUPER STATS

BUGATTI VEYRON SUPER SPORT
TOP SPEED: 267.81 mph (420.998 km/h)
0-60 MPH (0-100 KM/H): 2.5 seconds
FUEL ECONOMY (COMBINED):
    9.8 mpg (23.15 l/100 km)
HORSEPOWER: 1183 bhp
LENGTH: 175.6 in. (4462 mm)
WIDTH: 78.6 in. (1998 mm)
HEIGHT: 47.4 in. (1204 mm)
MADE IN: Germany
PRICE: $2.2 million

FORMULA ONE

If you love high-speed thrills and spills, then car racing is the place to be. The world's fastest, most pulse-pounding motorsports are Formula One and drag racing.

Big wheels give lots of grip.

Wings at the front and back of the car use the wind to help push the car down onto the track to improve grip.

Formula One is the most expensive and glamorous of all motorsports. These cars have powerful engines and lightweight bodies for tearing around tracks at high speed. Strict rules control what racing teams can do to their cars. Engineers try to find ways of making their cars even faster within these rules.

DRAG RACING

Dragsters need parachutes to help them slow down.

Dragsters have huge tires for plenty of grip.

Formula One may be quick, but drag racing is quicker. These cars sprint down a straight, quarter-mile- (400-m-) long track. They rocket along at over 330 mph (531 km/h). Dragsters have small, light front wheels and big rear wheels. Their engines run on a special fuel called nitro-methane.

SUPER STATS

RED BULL F1 CAR (OPPOSITE)

TOP SPEED: top secret, but over 200 mph (320 km/h)

0-60 MPH (0-100 KM/H): top secret (but estimated at around 2.5 seconds)

FUEL ECONOMY (ESTIMATED): 3.3 mpg (70.6 l/100 km)

HORSEPOWER: top secret (estimated at over 700 bhp)

LENGTH (ESTIMATED): 182.4 in. (4635 mm)

WIDTH (ESTIMATED): 70.8 in. (1800 mm)

HEIGHT (ESTIMATED): 37.4 in. (950 mm)

MADE IN: Austria

PRICE: not for sale

7

THRUST SSC

No car on Earth is faster—or rarer—than Thrust SSC. This unique wonder holds the land speed record. That means that it's not just the fastest thing on four wheels. It's the fastest thing on any number of wheels, legs... or even skis!

A normal car engine—even one from a supercar—couldn't hope to get Thrust to anywhere near its top speed. So engineers gave Thrust something different—two jet engines!

Thrust's driver was an ex-fighter pilot named Andy Green. At least he was used to the speed!

The engines are the same as those used on Phantom jet fighters.

The wheels are made from aluminum. There are no tires—they would fall apart at these high speeds.

Thrust SSC set the land speed record on October 15, 1997. The attempt took place at Black Rock Desert, Arizona. For a record to be official the car has to do two runs over a distance of a mile (1.6 km). The average speed of the two runs is taken. The average Thrust SSC achieved was a phenomenal 763.035 mph (1227.985 km/h)!

Many land speed record attempts happen in deserts like Black Rock. They are flat and dry—perfect conditions for speedy driving.

The engines sit either side of the driver's cabin.

The engines run on aviation fuel, the same stuff that powers jet planes.

SUPER STATS

THRUST SSC (SUPER SONIC CAR)
TOP SPEED: 771 mph (1240 km/h)
0-60 MPH (0-100 KM/H): Not known... but 0-100 mph (0-160 km/h) in 4 seconds
FUEL ECONOMY: unknown
HORSEPOWER: 110,000 bhp
LENGTH: 650 in. (16500 mm)
WIDTH: 146 in. (3700 mm)
HEIGHT: 90.5 in. (2300 mm)
MADE IN: Britain
PRICE: not for sale

The cockpit is a bit like a jet plane's and is designed to protect the driver from the force of the air rushing past.

LAMBORGHINI MIURA

The Lamborghini Miura was first built in 1968. It became an instant classic and these days many experts call it the world's first supercar. Why? Because it was stunningly beautiful, shockingly fast, and the engineering was very advanced for its time.

The radiator, fans, and spare wheel are under the hood.

The headlights rise up by roughly 30 degrees when switched on.

Marcello Gandini designed the bodywork. It was the first car he worked on—before that he had designed the insides of nightclubs!

Lamborghini started out making tractors, not cars—although farmers have never traveled as fast as this.

Like many supercars, the Miura is not very practical. It has little trunk space, the cabin is cramped, it's difficult to park, and you can hardly see out of the back. But—and it's a big but—it is also one of the most thrilling cars you can possibly drive. And that's what supercars are all about.

The engine is placed as near the middle of the car as possible to help the Miura stay balanced. Only racing cars had done this in the past.

The trunk is a small space left behind the engine.

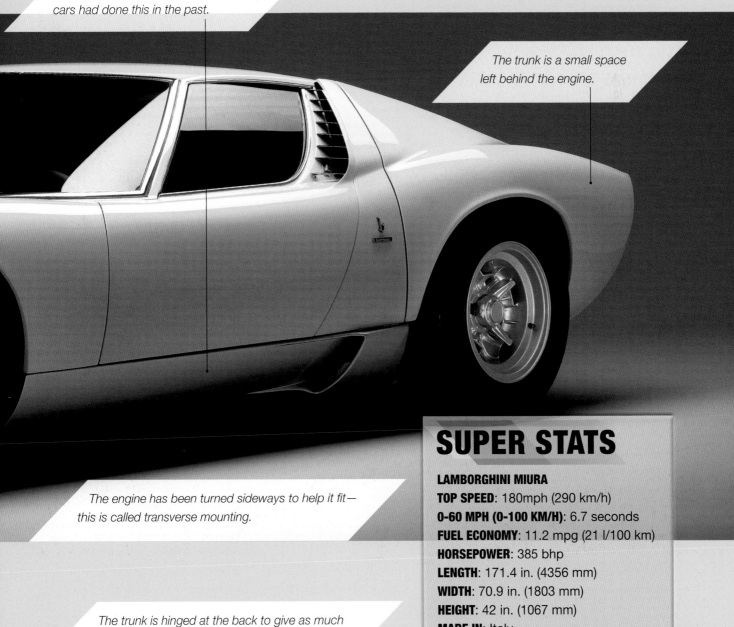

The engine has been turned sideways to help it fit—this is called transverse mounting.

The trunk is hinged at the back to give as much space as possible for working on the engine.

SUPER STATS

LAMBORGHINI MIURA
TOP SPEED: 180mph (290 km/h)
0-60 MPH (0-100 KM/H): 6.7 seconds
FUEL ECONOMY: 11.2 mpg (21 l/100 km)
HORSEPOWER: 385 bhp
LENGTH: 171.4 in. (4356 mm)
WIDTH: 70.9 in. (1803 mm)
HEIGHT: 42 in. (1067 mm)
MADE IN: Italy
PRICE: $26,000 (1970 price)

FERRARI 599 GTB

The Italian car firm Ferrari is perhaps the most famous of all the supercar makers. It started building racing cars in the 1940s, and by 1948 it also made road versions of these cars. The Ferrari symbol of a black horse goes hand in hand with the best supercars money can buy.

Lightweight aluminum body

HF07 CUV

The technology from Ferrari's Formula One racing cars is often found in their road cars. The Ferrari 599 is a good example of this. The driver changes gear by pressing paddles on the steering wheel. A computer helps to manage how the car handles on the road and how the suspension works. These ideas were both trialed in Formula One.

Inside, the cabin uses leather, aluminum, and carbon fiber for a lightweight but luxurious feel.

The 599 GTB is called a grand tourer. These cars are designed to travel long distances in style and comfort—and at speed! Unfortunately, because of their terrible fuel consumption, you'll need a hefty salary to travel far in a car like this.

Carbon fiber brakes

The rear tires are 0.98 in. (2.5 cm) bigger than the front tires.

SUPER STATS

FERRARI 599 GTB
TOP SPEED: Over 205 mph (330 km/h)
0-60 MPH (0-100 KM/H): 3.7 seconds
FUEL ECONOMY: 11.1 mpg (21.2 l/100 km)
HORSEPOWER: 612 bhp
LENGTH: 183.7 in. (4666 mm)
WIDTH: 77.2 in. (1960 mm)
HEIGHT: 52.6 in. (1336 mm)
MADE IN: Italy
PRICE: $283,700

ROLLS ROYCE
PHANTOM

Sometimes speed alone isn't enough. If you become a millionaire (good luck with that!), you might want something not just super-fast, but also super-luxurious. The Rolls Royce Phantom is one of the most luxurious supercars in the world.

The Phantom comes in 16 different colors. If you are willing to pay extra, Rolls Royce will make it any color you like.

Rolls Royce cars have a small metal statue of a woman at the front. She is called the Spirit of Ecstasy.

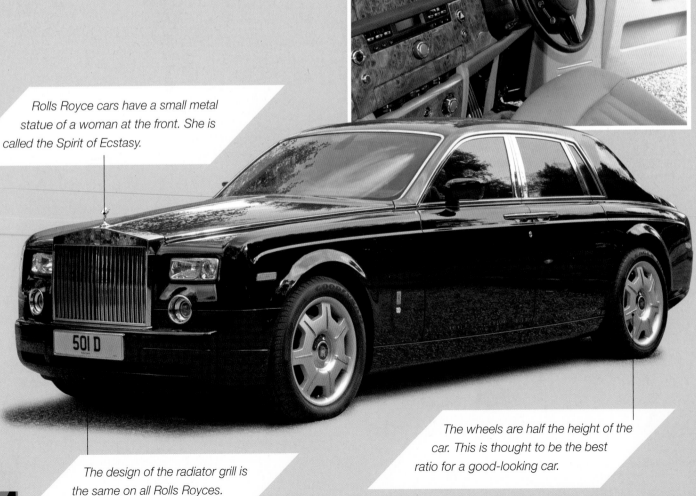

The wheels are half the height of the car. This is thought to be the best ratio for a good-looking car.

The design of the radiator grill is the same on all Rolls Royces.

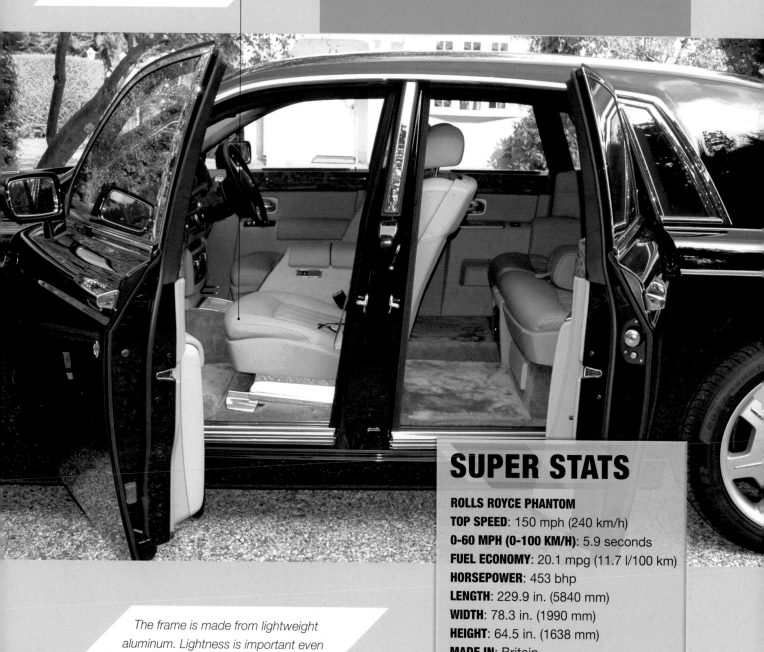

If buyers want more leg room in the back, they can get an extended version of the car, which is 9.8 in. (250 mm) longer.

About 180 ft. (55 m) of leather is used in the inside of the car.

Rolls Royce is one of the most famous names in the motoring world. The company was founded in 1904. Rolls Royce prides itself on making the most comfortable and quiet cars around. In the past, most Rolls Royce owners would have had chauffeurs. Today, the cars are so much fun to drive that most owners wouldn't let anyone else behind the wheel.

The frame is made from lightweight aluminum. Lightness is important even on big cars like the Phantom.

SUPER STATS

ROLLS ROYCE PHANTOM
TOP SPEED: 150 mph (240 km/h)
0-60 MPH (0-100 KM/H): 5.9 seconds
FUEL ECONOMY: 20.1 mpg (11.7 l/100 km)
HORSEPOWER: 453 bhp
LENGTH: 229.9 in. (5840 mm)
WIDTH: 78.3 in. (1990 mm)
HEIGHT: 64.5 in. (1638 mm)
MADE IN: Britain
PRICE: $456,000

MERCEDES SLS AMG

German company Mercedes-Benz has a very special place in motoring history. In 1885, Karl Benz built the world's first gasoline-powered motor car. Today his company is still ahead of the game and produces cars like the breathtaking SLS AMG.

The odd-looking doors are called gullwings. They look cool, but gullwing doors can be awkward to close, and if you park too close to something else, you're going to hit it.

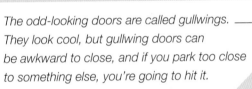

197 MBC

The SLS is the perfect combination of old and new. Its name and design hark back to the 1950s. However, its engineering is cutting edge. The engine has been tuned to be as powerful and as fast as possible.

The weight of the car is almost perfectly balanced between the front and back. A well-balanced car should handle better.

When the 300 SL was built in 1954, its makers claimed that it was the fastest road car in the world. It was also the first to use gullwing doors. It had these unusual doors because the shape of the body and the way it was made meant normal doors wouldn't fit.

The chassis and the body are made from lightweight aluminum, to keep the weight down.

SUPER STATS

MERCEDES SLS AMG
TOP SPEED: 197 mph (317 km/h)
0-60 MPH (0-100 KM/H): 3.8 seconds
FUEL ECONOMY: 17.8 mpg (13.2 l/100 km)
HORSEPOWER: 571 bhp
LENGTH: 182.5 in. (4638 mm)
WIDTH: 76.3 in. (1939 mm)
HEIGHT: 49.6 in. (1260 mm)
MADE IN: Germany
PRICE: $269,400

XENATEC MAYBACH COUPE

In the world of the supercar, there's no limit to how much cars can be modified. Engines can be tuned to make them more powerful. The interior and even the chassis can be transformed too. That's exactly what has happened with the Xenatec Maybach Coupe.

Customers can have a glass roof instead of the standard steel one if they want.

The inside of the car has thicker carpet than in most people's houses.

The original car that Xenatec modifies is a Maybach 57S. Maybach is the luxury brand belonging to Mercedes Benz.

The angles of the windshield and rear windows have been altered. Also, the pillars at the rear of the car have been moved farther back to make getting in and out easier.

German company Xenatec specializes in altering other manufacturers' cars. The Maybach coupe starts life as an already luxurious model from another company, called Maybach. Xenatec then makes it a little bit more special. The basic mechanics of the car stay the same, but the interior and exterior get a makeover.

Most of the exterior panels are different from those of the original car. Even the bumpers have been changed.

The original Maybach car has four doors but Xenatec rebuilds the body to make a sportier-looking two-door coupe.

SUPER STATS

XENATEC MAYBACH COUPE
TOP SPEED: 171 mph (275 km/h)
0-60 MPH (0-100 KM/H): 4.9 seconds
FUEL ECONOMY: 12.4 mpg (19 l/100km)
HORSEPOWER: 603 bhp
LENGTH: 225.5 in. (5728 mm)
WIDTH: 77.9 in. (1980 mm)
HEIGHT: 60.7 in. (1544 mm)
MADE IN: Germany
PRICE: $456,320

MEAN MACHINES

PAGANI ZONDA R

Some companies can never be satisfied in their quest for speed. The Pagani Zonda was one of the fastest and most fun-to-drive cars in the world. However, the perfectionists at Pagani obviously decided that it wasn't quite fast enough or fun enough—so they invented the Zonda R.

A big air scoop on the roof forces the wind over the engine to help keep it cool.

The tires are slick, which means they have no tread. These give more grip—unless it's raining, and then they are useless.

The suspension makes the ride smoother. On the Zonda R this can be adjusted to suit each individual driver.

The Zonda R was created for belting around a race track at blistering speeds. Racing circuits and test tracks sometimes allow sports car owners to bring their own vehicles along to give them a spin. The appeal is that you can drive your car at speeds way beyond those allowed on the roads.

Most of the car is made from either carbon or titanium—including the chassis. Carbon and titanium are both light and strong.

The wing can be adjusted to give more or less downforce.

The tires were made especially for this car by tire company Pirelli.

The engines are made by Mercedes Benz and have been tuned by AMG. The same engines have been used by Mercedes—in a racing car!

SUPER STATS

PAGANI ZONDA R
TOP SPEED: 171 mph (275 km/h)
0-60 MPH (0-100 KM/H): 2.7 seconds
FUEL ECONOMY: not known
HORSEPOWER: 750 bhp
LENGTH: 191.5 in. (4866 mm)
WIDTH: 79.2 in. (2014 mm)
HEIGHT: 44.9 in. (1141 mm)
MADE IN: Italy
PRICE: $2 million (estimated)

SHELBY TUATARA

When the Bugatti Veyron Super Sport became the world's fastest car, it took the crown from a small American company, Shelby Super Cars, and their SSC Ultimate Aero. Now Shelby wants the record back. This is the car they've built to do it: the Shelby Tuatara.

The body is made of carbon fiber.

The odd-looking winglets help provide downforce.

Even the wheels are made from carbon fiber.

Many of the details of the Tuatara have been kept top secret. We do know that the Tuatara will use the classic combination of power and lightness in its record attempt. The engine produces a staggering 1,350 bhp, and the car itself is mostly made from lightweight carbon fiber. Is it enough to beat the Veyron Super Sport? Only time will tell.

Added strength comes from aluminum crash supports. These will protect the car in any high-speed accidents.

The Tuatara is designed to be as aerodynamic as possible. This means that the air slips around the car when it moves. The more easily a car moves through the air, the faster it goes.

Grooves underneath the car use the passing air to help the car grip the road.

Big air scoops at the front, side, and rear of the car will cool the engine and create downforce.

SUPER STATS

SHELBY TUATARA
TOP SPEED: 275 mph (442 km/h) estimated
0-60 MPH (0-100 KM/H): 2.8 seconds estimated
FUEL ECONOMY: not known
HORSEPOWER: 1350 bhp
LENGTH: not known
WIDTH: not known
HEIGHT: not known
MADE IN: USA
PRICE: not known

BOWLER NEMESIS

Not all supercars are for tearing around race tracks or cruising around town. Some of them are designed to go places where normal machines fear to drive—such as off-road in deserts or forests. No car does this better than the Bowler Nemesis.

The Nemesis is wide and squat, but with plenty of space between the ground and the bottom of the car—perfect for off-roading.

The tires are big, chunky, and ideal for getting a grip on wet or slippery surfaces.

The Nemesis isn't any old off-roader. It is designed for high-speed, off-road racing. This takes it through some of the most difficult terrain in the world. You need a real supercar to compete in that, along with some pretty extraordinary modifications such as hydraulic rams, sand ladders, and fire extinguishers.

The Nemesis was designed to compete in the Dakar Rally. This race used to go from Paris, France to Dakar, Senegal. The last few years the race has been held in South America instead.

The body is made from carbon fiber and a material called Twin-tex.

An internal cage protects the driver if the Nemesis rolls over.

The trunk contains three spare wheels, sand ladders, tools, shovels, first-aid equipment, and spare water. You don't need all that to go shopping!

The car has a hydraulic ram fitted underneath. This is like a jack to push the car up off the ground if it gets stuck in the sand.

SUPER STATS

BOWLER NEMESIS
TOP SPEED: 140 mph (225 km/h)
0-60 MPH (0-100 KM/H): 5 seconds
FUEL ECONOMY: not known
HORSEPOWER: 257 bhp
LENGTH: 174.6 in. (4436 mm)
WIDTH: 78.7 in. (2000 mm)
HEIGHT: 68.1 in. (1730 mm)
MADE IN: Britain
PRICE: $262,750

NISSAN GT-R

Supercars don't have to be expensive—they just have to be special. Like its more costly rivals, the Nissan GTR looks remarkable. And it really is fast. The only difference between the GTR and most other supercars is that it can be yours for around half the price of the competition.

The GTR is a practical supercar. It has a big trunk and could easily carry home a family's supermarket shop.

The Japanese-built GTR may cost less than its European rivals. However, it's more than a match for them on the track. The GTR has excellent road-handling, a 0-60 time of just over 3 seconds and a top speed of 196 mph (315 km/h). There's not much that would beat it around a race track.

The Nissan GTR has four-wheel drive. This means that the engine powers all four wheels. Usually car engines only power two of the wheels.

Brembo fully ventilated drilled steel disc brakes

Independent Transaxle 4WD
GR6-type dual clutch transmission

Multi-structured body

VR38-type twin turbo engine

GT-R

Bilstein DampTronic dampers

Large-diameter run-flat tires

Premium Midship Package

"Run flat" tires can still be used even if they get a puncture.

The GTR's mighty engine has won it the nickname "Godzilla."

Scoops and vents in the hood help to cool the engine.

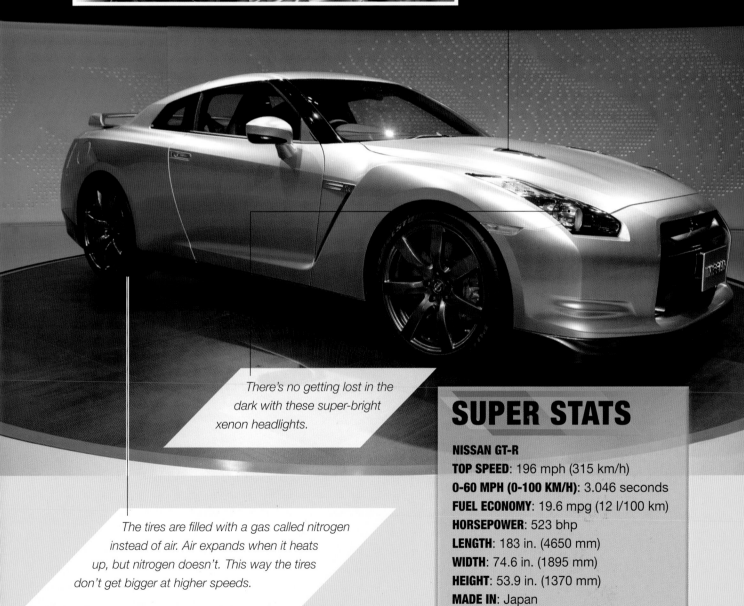

There's no getting lost in the dark with these super-bright xenon headlights.

The tires are filled with a gas called nitrogen instead of air. Air expands when it heats up, but nitrogen doesn't. This way the tires don't get bigger at higher speeds.

SUPER STATS

NISSAN GT-R
TOP SPEED: 196 mph (315 km/h)
0-60 MPH (0-100 KM/H): 3.046 seconds
FUEL ECONOMY: 19.6 mpg (12 l/100 km)
HORSEPOWER: 523 bhp
LENGTH: 183 in. (4650 mm)
WIDTH: 74.6 in. (1895 mm)
HEIGHT: 53.9 in. (1370 mm)
MADE IN: Japan
PRICE: $115,120

MEAN MACHINES

KOENIGSEGG AGERA R

Perhaps the biggest problem with supercars is the effect they have on the environment. Supercars use a lot of fuel. This results in exhaust gases that can help cause climate change. However, the Agera R is different—it uses biofuels, which produce fewer harmful gases. Now you can have a supercar and a clear conscience.

The tires are designed to cope with speeds of up to 260 mph (420 km/h).

The roof panel can be removed for open-top driving.

The wheels are designed to generate more downforce from the wind.

Super-fast cars need incredible brakes. The Agera R accelerates from 0 to 200 mph (322 km/h) and back in just under 25 seconds.

The Agera R doesn't just look amazing. There's lots of clever engineering here too. The car is made of carbon fiber and aluminum to keep it light for speed. Fast, light cars need lots of grip. The Agera gets its grip from smart use of wind, exhaust gases, and special wheels that create downforce.

The angle of the rear wing changes depending on how fast the air moves over it, for maximum effect.

Exhaust gases come out of vents in the rear pylons, which increase downforce.

The Agera R can run on gasoline, as well as biofuels.

The body is partly made from Kevlar—the same material that is used in bulletproof vests.

SUPER STATS

KOENIGSEGG AGERA R
TOP SPEED: 260+ mph (418+ km/h)
0-60 MPH (0-100 KM/H): 2.9 seconds
FUEL ECONOMY: 19.6 mpg (12 l/100 km)
HORSEPOWER: 1115 bhp
LENGTH: 169 in. (4293 mm)
WIDTH: 78.6 in. (1996 mm)
HEIGHT: 44.5 in. (1129 mm)
MADE IN: Sweden
PRICE: $1.5 million+ (estimated)

MEAN MACHINES

TESLA ROADSTER SPORT

In the past, the only road vehicle that put no exhaust gases into the air was a bicycle. Electric vehicles changed that, but they were slow and the batteries that provided the power ran out after just a few miles. Then came the Tesla Roadster: a supercar for the green generation.

The roadster gets its power from 6,831 lithium-ion batteries.

The batteries are rechargeable. You just plug the car in to charge it up.

The Tesla Roadster has everything you could want from a supercar. One thing is missing though: there's no engine noise. In common with all electric cars, the Roadster is as quiet as a mouse's sigh. The only noises you hear are the tires on the road and the wind rushing by.

The batteries charge each time the driver brakes, too.

Batteries last for seven years and have a range of 245 mi. (394 km) between charges.

Batteries are stacked behind the seats.

Electric cars might be green but they do have problems. It can take 13 hours to recharge the Roadster from a normal plug. This means trips of over 245 miles (394 km) are out of the question.

The body is hand made from carbon fiber panels.

Wheels are made from aluminum.

SUPER STATS

TESLA ROADSTER SPORT
TOP SPEED: 125 mph (201 km/h)
0-60 MPH (0-100 KM/H): 3.7 seconds
FUEL ECONOMY: does not apply
HORSEPOWER: 288 bhp
LENGTH: 155.1 in. (3939.5 mm)
WIDTH: 72.9 in. (1851.6 mm)
HEIGHT: 44.35 in. (1126.5 mm)
MADE IN: USA
PRICE: $145,000

GLOSSARY

aluminum a lightweight metal

bhp a measurement of the power of an engine. This stands for "brake horsepower."

biofuels fuels made from plants or other living things

carbon fiber a strong, light material made from thin rods of carbon. Carbon is also found in coal and diamonds.

chassis the base of a motor vehicle

coupe a car with two doors and a roof

downforce a force that pushes a car down into the road

hydraulic powered by a liquid forced through tubes under pressure

nitrogen a colorless gas that makes up most of the air

porcelain a hard material made by heating up crushed rocks and clay

sand ladder a wide, flat piece of metal that is used to spread the weight of a car tire and stop it getting stuck in sand

suspension the system in vehicles that stops passengers from feeling bumps

transverse positioned across something

xenon a gas used in electric lamps

FURTHER READING

Bullard, Lisa. *Ferrari (Blazers: Fast Cars)*. Capstone Press, 2007.

Editors of DK. *Car Crazy*. Dorling Kindersley, 2012.

Graham, Ian. *Fast Cars (How Machines Work)*. Saunders, 2011.

Hammond, Richard. *Car Science*. Dorling Kindersley, 2011.

Hampshire, Anthony. *Full Throttle (Redline Racing)*. Fitzhenry and Whiteside, 2005.

INDEX